AN OXFORD BESTIARY

New statue of Triton, Radcliffe Humanities Building

An Oxford Bestiary

Sophie Huxley

Photographs by Paul Freestone

HUXLEY SCIENTIFIC PRESS
OXFORD

Published by Huxley Scientific Press
35 Marston Street, Oxford OX4 1JU, UK
www.huxleyscientific.com

First published 2013

© Sophie Huxley 2013

Photographs © Paul Freestone 2013

ISBN: 978-1-909214-03-3

Designed and typeset in Minion by Geoff Ager
Printed and bound in the UK by Charlesworth Press, Wakefield

CONTENTS

Foreword vii

Introduction 1

The Bodleian Bestiaries 2

A Modern Bestiary 2

Quadrupeds 3

Birds 15

Reptiles 24

Insects 26

Sea Creatures 27

Mythical Beasts 28

Literary Creatures 33

A Congregation of Other Animals 34

Index 59

For Smokey and Albi

If we choose to let conjecture run wild, then animals, our fellow brethren in pain, diseases, death, suffering, and famine – our slaves in the most laborious works, our companions in our amusements – they may partake [of] our origins in one communal ancestor – we may be all netted together.

Charles Darwin, 'Notebooks on Transmutation', 1837

There is a certain Chinese encyclopedia entitled Celestial Emporium of Benevolent Knowledge *in the remote pages of which it is written that animals are divided into (a) those that belong to the Emperor, (b) embalmed ones, (c) those that are trained, (d) suckling pigs, (e) mermaids, (f) fabulous ones, (g) stray dogs, (h) those that are included in this classification, (i) those that tremble as if they were mad, (j) innumerable ones, (k) those drawn with a very fine camel-hair brush, (l) others, (m) those that have just broken a flower vase, (n) those that resemble flies from a distance.*

Jorge Luis Borges, 'The Analytical Language of John Wilkins', 1942

FOREWORD

A bestiary, as Sophie Huxley explains so clearly, was a medieval list or catalogue of animals, some quite familiar, others more exotic, and still others culled from fables and legends – animals which had never actually been seen by the writer or by any reader. The distinctive feature of the bestiary was that it was not content simply to describe the animal physically, but that it expounded each creature's moral, even spiritual, significance. The animal was regarded as a symbol of some characteristic that was also important in the human world: the fox represented cunning, the lion pride and strength, the ass humility and servitude. This is familiar enough and comes under the heading of folk wisdom. In the Christian Middle Ages, a deeper level of symbolism was introduced into the descriptions of fabulous creatures like the unicorn, which could be tamed or captured only by a virgin: this made it an emblem of Christ, who took on his human nature in a virgin's womb, and whose purity can be seen in the unicorn's whiteness. Another white creature and type of Christ was the charadrius bird, which was said to frequent royal courts and foretell the course of diseases. If the bird gazed fixedly at the patient, it would absorb the disease and fly up to the sun, where the evil would be burned away. Here the symbolism of the redemption from sin is clear; but if the bird turned its head away from the sufferer, the disease would be mortal.

    The fascination of this type of literature is that it appears to say that animals are part of God's world, that they are all there for a reason, and that they display God's wisdom and can reveal some truth to us, if we will listen. The same principle can be seen in the animal fables first attached to the name of Aesop, and rewritten over and over again down the centuries. The message of the fable was more practical, inculcating caution, prudence, and worldly wisdom, often by bringing two very different animals into confrontation. For example, a lion spares the life of an insignificant mouse, and later, when trapped in the hunters' nets, it is set free when the same mouse gnaws through the ropes, which the great and powerful lion was not equipped to do. The moral is that brute strength is not always the answer and that we all need friends. Such fables were retold in the seventeenth century in the subtle, refined, and musical language of Jean de La Fontaine.

These works, with their delightful illustrations, seemed again to reinforce the picture of humans and animals sharing the same world, not just physically but morally, as part of the harmonious order of nature in which we all have a place, a significance, and an ultimate value. These fables were regarded so highly that they provided the subjects for a series of sculptures, long since destroyed, in the grounds of the Palace of Versailles. Something of this sense that certain animals possessed some inherent meaning must clearly have been absorbed into the language of heraldry. The traditions of heraldry, of the bestiary, and of the fable explain why animal images were used for centuries as architectural features or whimsies.

This sense of harmony, of the integration of man and nature, was challenged and perhaps destroyed by the age of reason, and then by the age of science. Descartes had famously argued for the total separation between man and nature, proclaiming that animals were mere automata: they had no mind, no feeling, no soul. They were nothing but sophisticated machines, among whom we had to live, but whom we, as superiors, were free to use in any way we wished. This school of thought, the Enlightenment alienation of man from nature, the view of the world as a mere mechanism, had long-lived and damaging consequences as mankind moved into the age of science and the age of the machine. In the last half-century, reacting against this destructive teaching, we have set out once more to rediscover the ideal of equality and harmony between mankind and his environment, including the animals which once surrounded us but do so now in a far more fragile relationship. Sophie Huxley's book reminds us of the centuries during which the beauty, the humour, the strangeness, and the power of animals were constantly invoked in public images, especially in carvings.

But this is really a book with two themes: the first of course is the presence of animals in our lives, but the second is Oxford. Oxford is without doubt one of the most studied and analysed, described and depicted, pondered and dreamed-of cities in the world. Why is this? It can only be because Oxford has always been a place of ideas, of learning, of the intellect, and we desperately want to be part of it. We like to imagine that these qualities have merged into the physical environment, even into the air, and that this history is present, as Henry James said of Rome, 'in the stones of its streets and in the atoms of its sunshine'. This is the reason that we are so intent on studying the city's physical fabric, and also its legends and its characters – the nutty professors, wild-eyed poets, decadent aristocrats, and history-making statesmen who have created this atmosphere that we now breathe. These figures all helped to create the great traditions of the city and the university, and in a sense they form a kind of Oxford bestiary of their own: figures like Shelley, Lewis Carroll, Benjamin Jowett, Ruskin, Lord Curzon, Evelyn Waugh, C. S. Lewis, and so on, pass before us in imagination like the lions, the eagles, the unicorns, and the griffins of the medieval world. There have been many books about those iconic figures, but this book reveals a new aspect of Oxford. It inspires us to look again with fresh eyes at the buildings and the interiors of the city, whose artists and craftsmen show us that the animals are still with us; indeed, they have never gone away. This physical fabric brings the intellectual and the elemental down to earth, to carved stones, stained-glass windows, roof-beams, doorways, and inn signs. It was one of Oxford's most distinctive poets, Gerard Manley Hopkins, who spoke of Oxford's rural setting, its 'folk, flocks, and flowers', and who defined the city largely in terms of its birdsong when he described it as 'cuckoo-echoing, bell-swarmed, lark-charmed, rook-racked, river-rounded'.

But Hopkins was predominantly a poet of sky, birds, trees, clouds, air, and rainbow, and he had less to say about animals. If we want a more modern response to the rediscovery of nature, to the secrets that the animals know and we do not, we might turn to Pablo Neruda, a revolutionary poet in several senses:

If only I could speak with birds,
with oysters and with small lizards,
with the foxes of the dark forest,
with representative penguins,
if the sheep would listen to me,
the languorous woolly dogs,
the huge carriage horses, if only
I could talk things over with the cats,
if the chickens could understand me…

This sounds like a preliminary sketch for a modern bestiary, and it's something that Lewis Carroll would surely have identified with, as he would with Neruda's casual comment in the same poem, 'People are not enough.' Perhaps we do still see animals as guardian spirits of certain life-forces from which we have become estranged. If this is true, then this book will become a must for all animal watchers, showing us how the images of these guardian spirits have waited patiently through the centuries, and can now surprise and delight us in the most unexpected corners of Oxford.

Peter Whitfield
Charlbury
Oxfordshire
February 2013

AN OXFORD BESTIARY

INTRODUCTION

The habitat of Oxford takes in the rivers Thames and Cherwell and their flood plains. There is higher ground in Shotover to the east, Boar's Hill to the south and Wytham to the west. Carfax is at the top of the hill that falls to the Thames at the bottom of St Aldates, and to the Cherwell at the end of the High. The Thames arcs around Port Meadow and flows into Osney Island, an area protected by drains and channels that lead eventually back to the Thames. The Cherwell flows through north Oxford, with its blessed haven of water meadows, to pass under Magdalen Bridge and meet the Isis at the boathouses on Christ Church Meadow.

What animals and birds are and were here? What beasts in literature were inspired by the watery landscape? I have seen the Cherwell in winter with fog moving over the surface and expected at any moment to see a creature from the pages of Tolkien appear. The very name 'Oxford' introduces us to a crossing place over the Thames for cattle and we know our city to be a thousand years old. Animals are well represented in street and pub names. The arms of the colleges are full of heraldic beasts with meanings and connections throughout the country and through time. Alice's animals were deeply Oxford ones. Many colleges have mascots and pets belonging to the inhabitants that are recalled in stone. That Victorian triumph, the Oxford University Museum, is filled with preserved animals and also has the legendary dodo beak and foot, saved from a real dodo – now almost all that is left of an entire species. Everywhere on buildings and churches there are gargoyles – human, animal, and mythological. The Ashmolean Museum houses Renaissance animals so beautifully depicted they seem immediate and touchable.

The idea of a bestiary goes back to Greek civilization with Aesop's fables. The *Kalila wa Dimna* is an equivalent collection of animal tales in Arabic. In the Middle Ages stories about creatures were told that had moral teachings locked up in them. To explain these teachings, bestiaries were compiled in which accounts of beasts, birds, and fish were overlaid with moral and symbolic meanings.

THE BODLEIAN BESTIARIES

The medieval bestiaries in the Bodleian Library date from the thirteenth century and have direct links with ancient texts such as Pliny the Elder's *Natural History*. MS Bodley 764 and MS Ashmole 1511 are based on the *Physiologus*, which was written in Greek in the fourth century AD or earlier. The so-called 'B' Version in Berne is a Latin translation that dates from the eighth or ninth century AD. There are no extant Greek copies. Also important are the writings of Isidore of Seville (*c.* 560–636), particularly the *Etymologiae*, parts of which were copied into medieval bestiaries. There are thirteenth-century bestiaries whose illustrations are also derived from classical originals and are clearly to some extent copies of earlier works.

MS Ashmole 1511 contains an illustrated cycle of the Creation. This bestiary also includes work from the *Aviarium* (Book of Birds) of *c.* 1132–52 by Hugh of Fouilloy. Moral sentiments are expressed with the pictures, each of which is charming beyond belief and shows that the English love of animals was well developed by this time.

MS Bodley 764 shows working animals – a donkey by a watermill, a cow being milked, a cat chasing mice – as well as a wonderful green crocodile, a salamander, an elephant (Henry III had one in his menagerie), and birds such as a raven and a crow, as well as tame birds in a cage.

MS Ashmole 1511 is older, larger, and fancier than MS Bodley 764, but the latter has great appeal and also includes mythological beasts such as the unicorn and the dragon.

A MODERN BESTIARY

Oxford is full of animal connections, not least in its literature, its history, and its very name. A large cast of creatures both real and fantastical, past and present, rare and commonplace, is to be found in Oxford's colleges, churches, open spaces, gardens, museums, and buildings. They may be mere constructs of stone or glass, but the craftsman's skill brings them to life. They may be just parts of pub or street names, but they take us back to a quieter and gentler city.

QUADRUPEDS

Oxen can still be found on Christ Church Meadow, slowly chewing the cud and watching the tourists photographing them. The Thames must have been fordable from the earliest times and the cattle ate the lush grass of the water meadows and drank the river water. The ox is represented throughout Oxford on the city's coat of arms:

> Argent, an ox gules, its horns and hooves or, passing over a ford of three bars wavy azure and argent. (A red ox on a silver background with golden horns and hooves, passing over a ford of three wavy bars of blue and silver.)

One fine example of this is the shield with ox and stylized river on the old Oxford Boys' School on George Street, opposite the Odeon cinema. The former school is now part of the University.

Visitors arriving at the railway station will be struck by the statue of a huge bronze ox on a plinth by the Said Business School. This ox definitely means business: a strong, no-nonsense, look-at-me creature, he is letting

Figure 1 Bronze ox beside the Said Business School

everyone know that he represents the city. It is a pity for him he doesn't have a few bronze cows to keep him company.

Oxford town hall (1893, Henry Thomas Hare) is a masterpiece of Victorian architecture. It replaced the earlier Georgian town hall (1752), which itself replaced the Guildhall first built on this site in St Aldates in 1292. Particularly noteworthy is the plaster decoration of the main hall, with flourishes and curlicues in pastel colours. The building is adorned with animals, both heraldic and decorative. Over the main entrance an elephant and beaver support an ox. The elephant represents Sir Francis Knollys, High Steward of the City, and the green beaver is the badge of Henry Norreys, Captain of the Militia. The crest is topped by a half-lion, crowned and holding a Tudor rose. This crest was approved by Elizabeth I in 1566. Above, visible just below roof level, are the lion and unicorn, together with the royal coat of arms with the motto 'Dieu et mon droit'. On the roof line there are four dragons holding shields, with half-dragons supporting more decorative panels. At ground level (shoulder height) there are elephant heads. At the bottom of the staircase in front of you when entering the Town Hall are two dragons. Looking back down from the top of the stairs you can see a fully coloured arms of the City of Oxford. The beaver is green and the elephant is black with white chevrons (see front cover). The Victorian town hall cost £94,116 – far more than the original estimate of £50,000. A certain Alderman Underhill (Conservative) proclaimed that it would take fifty-five years until it 'ceased to be an incubus on the ratepayers'. Present-day 'ratepayers' will be familiar with the very many oxen depicted around the building because they appear on official notifications of an increase in council tax. Nothing changes!

✥

At Magdalen College, in the early eighteenth century, the formal walks were done away with and a deer park with fallow deer instituted. Surprisingly little is known about this from historical accounts or even tradition. In 1706 there is a record of payment 'for people killing deer in the grove'. In *Oxford in 1710* Zacharias von Uffenbach describes how 'at the back of Magdalen College, to the right of the college is a park belonging to it, a pleasant spot. There are numerous white and other stags and deer amongst which two, white spotted with brown, were as beautiful and tame creatures as I ever saw.' The 1787 *Oxford Almanac* shows deer in front of the New Building, while an earlier account from 1747 reports: 'They have converted the grove into a paddock, which feeds about twenty head of deer and there is a very fine bowling green on one side of it.' Magdalen is more like a grand country house than an ordinary Oxford college. Mr Allen of Tubney Wood, who delivers logs to us, says he used to cull the deer in the deer park from Magdalen tower with a rifle. Apparently students used to make the deer drunk with port-soaked sugar.

At the time of writing, one of the feral roe deer in Christ Church Meadow has taken to jumping the fence and eating all the herbaceous plants in the Memorial Gardens. It is getting very tame and particularly likes eating asters.

In the winter of 2012–13 five feral roe deer were grazing on the rugby pitch in Christ Church Meadow. They had jumped the fence and could easily be seen from Deadman's Walk.

❖

In Broad Street, outside Balliol College, below the Oriel window, the oak and lion image is the crest of Miss Hannah Brackenbury, who funded the rebuilding of the south and east ranges of the front quad in the 1860s. The motto 'Oncques Sans Reculer Jamais' is in archaic French and means approximately 'Never, ever give up.'

Brasenose College is named after a brazen (that is, bronze or brass) door knocker in the shape of a nose. A bronze door knocker that dates from the fourteenth century hangs in Hall

Figure 2 Balliol College crest

AN OXFORD BESTIARY

Figure 3 Lion door knocker, Kettell Hall

over the High Table, but it is in the shape of a lion's or a leopard's face. There is an intriguing story behind this knocker. In 1890 a house in Stamford, Lincolnshire, was offered for sale. Because Stamford had been the home of rebellious Oxford students, including one 'Phillipus le manciple ate Bresnose' in the 1330s, the Victorian dons imagined that the knocker on the door of this house, which was known as 'Brasenose', was the original one from Brasenose Hall in Oxford, taken there by the students. So the dons purchased the house and brought the knocker back to the college, where it can be seen to this day.

Kettell Hall, between Blackwell's and the cottages that form the entrance to Trinity College, was built around 1620. Ralph Kettell (1599–1643) was President of Trinity. The house is of stone and the front door is original, with its magnificent lion doorknocker.

On the west side of Folly Bridge Island, Nos. 1 and 2 date from the late 1840s. There is a terracotta lion in front of this house.

The Morrell's Brewery site near the castle has two golden half-lions holding flowers.

'Catte Street' is a rendering of the medieval name 'Cat Street'. This became 'Catherine Street' in the

Figure 4 Morrell's Brewery lion

nineteenth century before getting its present name. It was also known as 'Kattestreete' in the thirteenth century and 'Mousecatcher's Lane' ('Vicus Murilegorum' in English medieval Latin) in 1442. The medieval apothecaries' quarter was what is now Radcliffe Square, and the Physic School in Catte Street survived until 1485.

Beaumont Palace stood at the western end of Beaumont Street. Richard the Lionheart and King John were born there. In 1318, during the reign of Edward II, a clerk from Oxford called John Deydras came to the palace and tried to convince people that he was the king. Moreover, he said that his cat was the Devil and had persuaded Deydras that he was royal. Deydras was hanged for sedition (agitation against the authority of the state) and, as was common in medieval times, the cat was executed too. Animals were often punished, being thought to be possessed by evil spirits, or associated with witches.

The coat of arms of Jesus College, which has always had strong Welsh connections, shows three stags trippant, but the origins of their presence there is uncertain. More interesting is the fact that one principal of Jesus College, Joseph Hoare, was killed by his cat. Principal from 1768 to 1802, Hoare was profoundly deaf and one fateful day he inadvertently trapped his cat's tail beneath his chair. Because he could not hear its cries, the cat in desperation scratched his leg. The wound became infected and the Principal died of septicaemia, aged ninety-five.

In Corpus Christi College, by the new auditorium, there is a tombstone to a cat called Tom.

The royal coat of arms above the main entrance to the Sheldonian has an unusual lion and unicorn. The building was completed in 1669. There is a large lion and unicorn and royal arms on the High Street side of Brasenose College.

⁜

Professor Sir David Macdonald studied foxes in East Oxford during the 1970s and 80s. His method was to catch a fox (not the easiest of things to do) and fit it with a radio-transmitting collar. Using an old black taxi with an aerial on its roof, the research team would drive up and down Cowley Road and the surrounding streets taking radio fixes on a fox and calculating its whereabouts. Macdonald's work was a classic of its kind and revealed the secret life of the urban fox in an unforgettable way. Radio-tracking is now a standard way of following animals in their environment.

In the 1675 Loggan print of Corpus Christi College there is a fox chained up in the kitchen yard. Fox was the name of the founder of Corpus, and in 1512 Henry VIII said to the Spanish ambassador that he 'was a foxe indeed'. There is a record of expenditure of 10d for 'a chain for ye foxe'. The fox can be seen as symbolizing worldly skills. Carvings in medieval churches often show a fox preaching to foolish fowls – in this case it was seen as a sly and hypocritical beast.

Figure 5 Fox in James Street

❖

The dogs on the coat of arms of Lady Margaret Hall represent the dogs on the arms of Edward Stuart Talbot. Lady Margaret Hall was founded in 1878 by Talbot and his wife, Lavinia. He was an Anglican bishop and the first warden of Keble College. In heraldry a Talbot dog is a large white hound and these hounds appear on the shield of the Earls of Shrewsbury, whose family name is Talbot and to whom Edward was related.

The Angel and Greyhound pub is a new creation in an older building. This pub is named after two meadows called the Angel and the Greyhound between St Clement's and the Cherwell. These meadows were used to graze horses brought down from the old Angel and Greyhound coaching inns on the High Street.

On the tower of St Peter-in-the-East is a gargoyle, carved by Michael Groser, of the former Dean and Chaplain of St Edmund Hall, the Rev. Graham Midgley, and his dog, Fred.

Beneath this turf the Dean's dog Fred
Without his master goes to Earth, stone dead.
But on the tower, stone Dean and Fred together
Enjoy the sunshine and endure bad weather.

In 1656 an experiment took place in the gardens of Wadham College when Wilkins, Wren, and Boyle injected sack wine and opium into a dog. The dog had to be whipped to keep him from falling into a coma, so quickly did the drugs take effect. Intravenous drug use had not been studied before and this is probably the first recorded experiment of its kind.

Figure 6 Dean Midgley and Fred, St Edmund Hall

Robert Gunther's *Oxford Gardens* (1912) shows the position in the Botanic Garden of two large cement sculptures of a dog and a boar, both of which have antique Greek and Roman models from which they are artistically descended. The boar was removed in 1956, having been irreparably damaged by frost and wheelbarrow collision, while the dog was taken to the University Surveyor's yard, where it remains to this day.

The dog is sitting on its haunches with its mouth open, showing its teeth. The Roman writer Lucretius talks about Molossian hounds, which are very fierce: 'When the large loose lips of the Molossian dogs start to snarl in anger, baring their hard teeth … they threaten with a noise far other than when they bark … yet when they essay fondly to lick their cubs with their tongue … they fondle them with a growling voice' (*De Rerum Natura*, Book 5, line 1063). There was a famous ancient Greek statue of a Molossian hound that was brought as a trophy of war to Rome by the general Lucius Aemilius Paullus when he sacked Epirus in north-west Greece in 168 BC. The statue was much admired and copied in Rome and a version came from there to England as a result of one young man's Grand Tour in 1755–60. The proud owner was 'Dog' Jennings, who called it 'The Dog of Alcibiades' because of its truncated tail (the statesman Alcibiades cut off his dog's fine tail to give the people of Athens something else to talk about other than Alcibiades himself). Jennings's dog is now in the British Museum.

This prototype was copied in the 1840s by the firm Austin and Seeley in a concrete mix as a garden ornament and it is from here that our dog and boar must have come. The boar has classical associations too. In Homer, Artemis, the Goddess of the Chase, sent a wild boar to devastate the lands of King Oeneus of Calydon. It was eventually killed by Meleager, the king's son. Our boar is a copy of a fifth-century-BC original in the Uffizi Gallery, Florence. There is also a 'Bacchic Vase' with two goats' heads as handles, which appears in an Austin and Seeley catalogue of 1844, as do the dog and boar.

There were two sphinxes in the Botanic Garden, one a Roman original and the other a matching copy, which were replacements for the dog and boar. They were removed to the Egyptian Gallery of the Ashmolean Museum.

⁘

There is a wonderful apocryphal story concerning a student of Queen's College called Copcot, who one day was taking a stroll through Shotover Park. He had with him a volume of Aristotle, which he had been struggling, without success, to understand. Suddenly he was attacked by a wild boar, but with great presence of mind he shoved the book down the beast's throat, exclaiming in Latin *'Graecum est'* – roughly, 'It's all Greek to me!' Whereupon the boar choked to death on the undigestible work. It is not known where this story comes from, but the Copcots were an influential family from Horspath, a village to the east of Oxford, in the fifteenth and sixteenth centuries and tradition has it that the last wild boar in England was killed on the Shotover estate. There is a painting outside the Upper Library at Queen's of John Copcot and an eighteenth-century stained-glass window at Horspath Church also shows him.

The Boar's Head Ceremony at Queen's College, which was originally held on Christmas Day, can be traced back to the fourteenth century and a payment for wild boar appears in college accounts for 1395–6. The ceremony is thought to be Viking in origin and may have come down with members of the college from Cumberland and Westmorland. A boar was provided every year from 1585 by tenants in Bramley, Hampshire. In 1958 it was decided that college servants should not have to work on Christmas Day, so the ceremony became a Gaudy held on the Saturday preceding Christmas. Before the meal a boar's head is carried into the Dining Hall by the chefs to be presented to the Provost and Fellows at High Table. The choir follows behind in procession, singing the Boar's Head Carol. The head chorister is given the orange from the boar's mouth by the Provost. He and the Fellows then hand out sprigs of holly painted gold to the guests. The lyrics of the carol are:

The boar's head in hand bring I
Bedeck'd with bays and rosemary
I pray you, my masters, be merry.
Quot estis in convenio [As many as are in the feast].

(Chorus)
Caput apri defero [The boar's head I offer].
Reddens laudes Domino [Giving praises to the Lord].

The boar's head, as I understand
Is the rarest dish in all this land
Which thus bedeck'd with a gay garland
Let us *servire cantico* [serve with a song].

(Chorus)

Our steward hath provided this
In honour of the King of Bliss,
Which on this day to be served is
In Reginensi atrio [In the Queen's Hall].

AN OXFORD BESTIARY

The large plaster cast of a boar taken from a work in the Uffizi Gallery in Florence was given to Queen's College in 1774. It is now in the cast gallery of the Ashmolean Museum.

✣

At the junction of Alfred Street, Bear Lane (so named since at least 1814) and Blue Boar Street lies the Bear Inn, with its famous collection of neckties. The timber-framed three-storey building was built in 1606 as an ostler's house for a much larger inn that ran from the High Street to the corner where the modern Bear now stands. This large inn, called Parne Hall, burned down in 1421, was rebuilt as Le Tabard and became the Bear in 1432, retaining that name until 1801. It probably comes from the Bear and Ragged Staff on the coat of arms of Richard Neville, Earl of Warwick (1428–71). It was a large and important meeting place both for circuit judges and Royal Commissions. In 1586 some students had a fight with Lord Norris and his entourage there over the prosecution of some Magdalen men who had poached a deer from Shotover Royal Forest. The Bear was also a very well-known coaching inn, with impressive facilities – there were thirty rooms and stabling for thirty horses at the start of the nineteenth century.

Blue Boar Street runs along the northern wall of Christ Church to St Aldates. It used to be called Tresham's Lane after the person responsible for

Figure 7 The Bear Inn, Blue Boar Street

enclosing the road to the south (Christ Church land). It was also known as Little Jewry or Jury Lane because this was the medieval Jewish quarter. In the seventeenth century 'the Blewebore' House stood here and it is claimed that this is how the street got its name.

⸸

The White Horse pub, with Blackwell's on either side, has a modern front attached to a sixteenth- or seventeenth-century building. It is very small and cosy, and one sits inside below street level. There is a possible connection with the original name for Broad Street, which was known as Horsemonger Street around 1230: horses were bought and sold here. Another name is 'Canditch', referring to the ditch outside the city wall which ran along the southern edge of Broad Street.

The Old Black Horse Inn is a seventeenth-century coaching inn, now run as a pub and hotel. It is a few seconds' walk from the Plain, across Magdalen Bridge from the city. The old stables and carriage stores have been converted into accommodation.

Just next to the tower of St Martin at Carfax is an arch with a copper scene of St Martin and the beggar. The horse is a fine specimen and an equally fine one can be seen in the Eric Gill bas-relief of the same subject at Campion Hall, in Brewer Street.

⸸

The Turf Tavern was originally known, engagingly, as the Spotted Cow. The building had been here since about 1650, with eighteenth- and nineteenth-century additions. It is still a good place for a pint, and food is served as well. It lies just outside the city wall (1226–40), with New College to one side.

⸸

Of all the unlikely pets for a gardener, the German botanist Jacob Bobart the Elder (1599–1680) favoured a goat. Bobart had come to England to be the first head gardener at the Botanic Garden (then known as the Oxford Physic Garden). He and the goat are shown in a woodcut standing in front of the Danby Arch, the goat looking quizzically at Bobart. The same image also appears on an eighteenth-century imported Chinese porcelain plate displayed in the Ashmolean. Perhaps Bobart had trained his goat not to eat the plants!

❖

Agnus Dei, the Lamb of God, appears in many places but one particularly good example is at the base of a fifteenth-century brass monument in the choir at Merton Chapel. It is a double memorial to John Bloxham, Warden, wearing a gown and hood, and beside him to John Whytton, Rector of Wood Eaton, wearing a cassock and hood. They are enclosed by a small double canopy and underneath is the Agnus Dei. In the Christian Church the Lamb and Flag is a very well-known symbol. In St John's Gospel the sentences 'Behold the Lamb of God which taketh away the sin of the world' (1:29) and 'Behold the Lamb of God' (1:36) connect Jesus with the lamb. The sacrificial death of Jesus mirrors the very ancient custom of killing an animal to atone for one's sins. Jesus is 'he who takes away the sin of the world'. Usually the lamb is shown supporting a cross, or a banner with a red cross on a white ground, with his front right leg and shoulder visible. The Lamb and Flag also represents St John himself.

The pub of the same name at Nos. 12 and 13 St Giles belongs to St John's College, to which it is adjacent. The college uses its profits (£50,000 p.a.) to fund PhD students. Thomas Hardy's novel *Jude the Obscure*, which tells of a poor student failing to succeed in Oxford, was apparently mostly written in this pub. Graham Greene mentions the pub in his autobiography and it has been filmed for the *Inspector Morse* TV series. The building has been a pub

Figure 8 The Lamb & Flag, St Giles

since 1695 and still retains some eighteenth-century features. According to a survey in 1772, No. 12 was occupied by a Mrs Hicks and No. 13 by a Mr Williams. St John's had bought No. 12 from Godstow Abbey. There are excellent records (the census and directories) of who lived in the pub and the sort of wheeler-dealer business that took place there, including auctions for houses and horses, land and tolls.

⁘

Charles Daubeny, Professor of Chemistry and Botany and Keeper of the Botanic Garden, kept monkeys in a cage in the Danby Arch of the Botanic Garden, which were shown to guests after dinner. 'One night it was found that the door had been forced and the monkeys liberated. The professor was much vexed, but did not discover the culprit, whom Tuckwell believed to be Harry Wilkins of Merton. The monkeys were captured the next day, wandering dismal on the Iffley Road, or perched *crepitantes dentibus* [with teeth chattering] on the railings in Rose Lane'.

According to Descartes, monkeys could speak if they wanted to but keep silent so that they will not be made to work.

BIRDS

A bestiary compiled by Leonardo da Vinci describes the pelican thus: 'It is greatly devoted to its young and, finding them in the nest killed by snakes, tears at its breast, bathing them with its blood to bring them back to life.'

For such a small college, Corpus Christi is exceptionally rich in iconography. There is a striking pelican, standing proudly on top of the Turnbull sundial in the middle of the main quad.

Figure 9 Pelican, Corpus Christi College

AN OXFORD BESTIARY

Painted gold, it shines magnificently in the sunshine. The pelican is plucking its breast so that drops of blood fall on to its chicks below. This symbolizes Christ feeding the Church with spiritual nourishment, the pelican standing for piety and the Eucharist. There is another pelican on Merton Street on the Jackson annexe.

❖

Elizabeth Wordsworth, who founded St Hugh's in 1886, named the college in honour of her father, who, like St Hugh (1140–1200), was a bishop of Lincoln. St Hugh's symbol is the swan of Stow. This was a real, true, historical swan, as described by Giraldus Cambrensis. On the day that Hugh was enthroned at Lincoln Cathedral a great swan appeared at his manor at Stow. He killed all other male swans and spared only one female. Its beak was straight and yellow (i.e. a whooper swan). When the Bishop arrived, it became friendly and tame, taking bread from his hand. It would mutter as if talking to him. The swan seemed to know when its master was about to return and kept other people from him by honking and flapping its wings. It guarded Hugh when he was asleep. This continued for thirteen years, until the swan refused all contact and behaved like a sick creature, as if portending death. Six months later Hugh died. At St Hugh's there is a statue of the saint with his swan in the library. In fact there are many representations of swans around the college but the finest are the Swan Gates in Canterbury Road, designed in 1986, the college's centenary, by Laurence Whistler, who is best known as a glass engraver, and forged by Richard Quinnell, a master craftsman in iron.

❖

Figure 10 The Blackbird, Blackbird Leys

The Blackbird is a community pub in Blackbird Leys with a mainly Afro-Caribbean clientele. Blackbird Leys was built in the 1960s to house people from the demolished St Ebbe's slum housing and people from overseas who had come to Oxford to live.

❖

Martlets are heraldic birds, traditionally without legs and having only a tuft of feathers in their place. They are identified with swifts and, like them, they never land. This is symbolic of the restless quest for knowledge and in Oxford martlets appear in the coats of arms of both University College and Worcester College.

Although it is now agreed that University College owes its origins to the benefaction of William of Durham, who died in 1249, a legend grew up in the 1380s (fostered by the college, to assist them in getting royal support in a complex court case) that University College had been founded by King Alfred. The legend took root and by the sixteenth century University College had begun to adopt Alfred's coat of arms, or at least those arms attributed to him. These included the martlets. It is not known when the college started using these bogus arms of a bogus founder, but they certainly were by 1574, when heralds visited Oxford. Either four or five martlets can be used; designs vary, but sometimes a fifth is put alongside, or shown flouncing off in a temper!

❖

Like many of the older colleges, St Edmund Hall is associated with scholars from a particular part of the country. For Welshmen it is Jesus College, but for St Edmund Hall it is Cornwall. Two early principals were from Cornwall and many Cornishmen studied there before returning home to their native land. Cornwall is forever linked with the chough, a black corvid (*Pyrrhocorax pyrrhocorax*) slightly smaller than a crow, which makes a characteristic 'chuff' noise and has a long, curved, red beak and red legs. Choughs nest on rocky cliffs which abound there by the sea and are more frequent now than they were some years ago, but are still relatively few in number. Choughs also appear in the Arthurian legends: it is said that King Arthur's soul migrated into a chough when he died. The arms of St Edmund Hall show four choughs around a cross, while the sundial in the main quad has a chough

Figure 11 Chough on sundial, St Edmund Hall

painted on the background. Like magpies and jackdaws, choughs have a fondness for bright, shiny objects, which they regard with eyes that have a red and blue iris.

❖

Magpie Lane connects the High Street with Merton Street and hence Christ Church Meadow. Turning off the High through a dark passage that descends past ancient houses on the left and the high walls of Oriel to the right, the lane branches left (now Kybald Street) to the sixteenth-century house called Kybald Twychen, which boasts a monstrous door knocker. This house was a brothel and in medieval times Magpie Lane was originally known by the vulgar name Gropecunt Lane. The 'Magpie' nomenclature came from an ale house of that name. It was also called Grope Street and Grove Street. However, by 1930 it had become once and for all Magpie Lane. Corpus Christi College knocked down some delightful cottages and built 'New Building' in their place in the 1970s. Magpie Lane is also the name of a well-known group of Oxfordshire folk musicians, with many recordings to their credit.

⁂

In referring to the Four Evangelists in his *Book of Imaginary Beings*, Jorge Luis Borges describes their symbols:

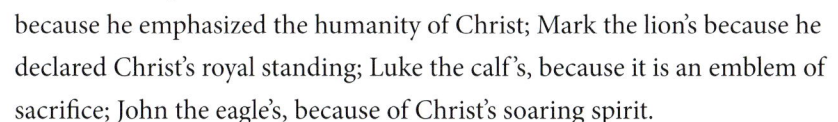

Figure 12 Knocker on Kybald Twychen, Kybald Street

> Matthew was given the man's face because he emphasized the humanity of Christ; Mark the lion's because he declared Christ's royal standing; Luke the calf's, because it is an emblem of sacrifice; John the eagle's, because of Christ's soaring spirit.

The brass lecterns to be seen in college chapels date from as early as around 1500 at Merton and 1617–18 at Jesus. The Merton lectern has a gabled book-rest, but others are in the form of an eagle supporting a Bible on its back, wings spread. The pedestal is stabilized by three or four feet in the shape of lions. Corpus Christi College owns an early sixteenth-century lectern; the rest are seventeenth-century (Magdalen, 1633; Exeter, 1637; Balliol, 1635; Queen's, 1653; Oriel, 1654 and Wadham, 1691).

The fourteenth-century founder of Queen's College was Robert d'Eglesfield, whose arms show three eagles, the first of which has a gold star on its breast. Eglesfield is a village in Cumberland and the college has many connections with the north of England. There is a large sculpture of an eagle on the college library, viewable from Queen's Lane.

The Eagle and Child pub in St Giles, opposite the Lamb and Flag, is a stone and timber-framed building probably built in the late seventeenth century, but the front is modern. It was owned from the seventeenth century by University College, but was bought in 2003 by St John's College for £1.2 million. By repute it was the Exchequer for Charles I's army, but this does not tie in with the earliest date for the building, which is 1650. The first mention of the name 'Eagle and Child' occurs in 1684. It might be connected with the legend that Zeus in the form of an eagle snatched the beautiful boy Ganymede and took him to Olympus to be a cup-bearer for the gods. The name Ganymede is corrupted into Latin and English as 'catamite'. Another possibility is that the name comes from the arms of the Earl of Derby, which have a coronet with the eagle and child. The pub was also known (certainly in the 1920s) as 'the Bird and Baby' and indeed as 'the Fowl and Foetus'. It is best known as the meeting place of the Inklings, a group of friends including C. S. Lewis, J. R. R. Tolkien, Charles Williams, Neville Coghill, and H. V. D. Dyson, who met from the 1930s to the 1960s to enjoy each other's company and discuss their literary efforts. The Eagle and Child retains some cosy booths at the front, but the 'Rabbit' room, where the Inklings met, has been changed.

❖

'As for a preposterous ritual, no event in Europe can be much sillier, not the most footling country frolic or pointless Anatolian orgy, than the Ceremony of the Mallard at All Souls' – Jan Morris, *Oxford*

The Mallard Song is sung on All Souls' Day at the November Gaudy. On 14 January (St Hilary's Day) there is a mallard procession once a century (the last in 2001). There are several recordings of the song; what follows here combines all the different verses. The first and last verses refer to the feast and the others to the prodigious nature of the bird.

The Griffine, Bustard, Turkey & Capon
Lett other hungry Mortalls gape on
And on theire bones with Stomacks fall hard,
But lett All Souls' Men have ye Mallard.

(Chorus)
Hough the bloud of King Edward,
By ye bloud of King Edward,
It was a swapping, swapping mallard!

Some storys strange are told I trow
By Baker, Holinshead & Stow
Of Cocks & Bulls, & other queire things
That happen'd in ye Reignes of theire Kings.

(Chorus)

The Romans once admir'd a gander
More than they did theire best Commander,
Because hee saved, if some don't foolle us,
The place named from ye Scull of Tolus.

(Chorus)

The Poets fain'd Jove turn'd a Swan,
But lett them prove it if they can.
To mak't appeare it's not att all hard:
Hee was a swapping, swapping mallard.

(Chorus)

Hee was swapping all from bill to eye,
Hee was swapping all from wing to thigh;
His swapping tool of generation
Oute swapped all ye wingged Nation.

(Chorus)

Then lett us drink and dance a Galliard
in ye Remembrance of ye Mallard,
And as ye Mallard doth in Poole,
Lett's dabble, dive & duck in Boule.

(Chorus)

To provide some elucidation… In the first verse, the griffin is a fabulous and heraldic creature with the body of a lion and the wings and head of an eagle. Bustards (which have been reintroduced on Salisbury Plain) were eaten, as were turkey (from 1555) and capon (chicken). Griffin is not said to be eaten in any mythological tale, but it sounds good in the song. In the chorus, 'hough' and 'ho' mean the same thing and 'swapping' means whopping great. In the second verse, 'Cocks & Bulls' refers to talking boastful rubbish. In the third verse, the mention of 'a gander' refers to the geese that alerted the Romans to a Gaulish attack on the Capitol in 390 BC (a caput or skull had been found there, hence 'skull of Tolus' mentioned by the Roman historian Livy). The fourth verse refers to the story of Leda, who was made love to by Zeus in the form of a swan. In the final verse 'Boule' means 'bowl'. So, drinking from a bowl like a mallard on the pond, the Lord Mallard is carried in a chair, with a mallard carried on a long pole before him, around the quad with flaming torches to the singing of 'The Mallard Song'.

In the seventeenth century the younger men of the Fellowship knocked on doors and demanded money. In early November the ceremony ends with a feast. In January Mallard Night was more of an initiation ceremony for young Fellows. Thomas Hearne (1678–1735) wrote: 'They tell you that the occasion for this [mallard] song was a mallard grown to a prodigous bigness that was found in a sink when the workmen were preparing it. It had continued there for several years – I think almost since the first foundation of the college for about twenty years current or more. In commemoration of the fact they sing this song with much mirth for a whole night together being All Souls' Night, every year.'

The Oxford antiquarian Anthony à Wood (1632–95) gives a brief description of the Mallard Night. His book was called *Histories and Antiquities of Oxford*. A copy of this was owned by Alderman William Fletcher (1739–1826) which he donated to the Bodleian in 1818. After the All Souls section Fletcher gives an inaccurate account of the Mallard Night and underneath is a card having the wax impression of William Mallard's seal. Fletcher has written underneath 'Impression of a seal found by some workmen in digging a drain on the site of All Souls College eastwards of the Warden's lodgings.' The seal represents a griffin, with the lettering *S. Guil. Malardi Clici (Sigillum Guillielmi Malardi Clerici)* or *Seal of William Mallard, clerk*. It is cut in a thirteenth-century style. Edward I was the great king of the thirteenth and fourteenth centuries. If the seal had been found in the seventeenth century, and some college wit had combined William Mallard of the seal with a story of a gigantic mallard found in a drain at the college's foundation, this could explain the legend and the song. Baker, Hollingshead, and Stow were writing chronicles of England, Scotland and Ireland and of their kings in the sixteenth and seventeenth centuries – clearly later than the founding of All Souls in 1437.

✣

Magdalen has had swans since at least 1490, when their keeper received 3s 1d for caring for and feeding them. That same year the Queen accepted a swan and a peacock from the college. In 1904 the Vintners' Company of London, who partly own the swans on the Thames, presented Magdalen with a pair of black swans to commemorate the Master of the Company, who was also a Magdalen man. In 1917 an old male black swan was trapped by unfamiliar ice at Folly

AN OXFORD BESTIARY

Bridge. Later he seduced the female of another pair of black swans (again from the Vintners'). They nested and produced six grey cygnets from a nest below Iffley lock.

❖

Bishop Oldham, co-founder of Corpus Christi College, had as his badge the owl. An owl teaspoon is given by the college to long-serving members of staff, while owls and the pelican appear on the college's coat of arms.

In 1884 Magdalen received the gift of an emu, which soon died from being overfed with currant cake.

In 1894 Lord Rothschild offered ostriches for the Magdalen Grove, but these were refused.

REPTILES

The arms of St Hilda's College contain a coiled serpent, which represents St Hilda. She turned a plague of snakes at Whitby into stone, according to legend – this is the story that local people told when trying to explain the spiral

Figure 13 Owl on sundial

ammonite fossils that they found in the cliffs and beaches there. According to a seventeenth-century writer: 'In that monasterie of Whitby, there were such an abundance of serpents, what throughe the thickness of bushes, and the wildnesse of the woods that the virgins durst not peepe out of their cells, or goe to draw water. But by her prayers, she obtained of god, that they might be turned into stones, yet so as the shape of serpents still remayned; which to this day, the stones of that place do declare, as eye-witnesses have testified.'

⁜

To the Chinese the heavens are hemispherical and the earth is quadrangular. In the tortoise, with its curved upper shell and flat lower shell, they find a model of the world. Soothsayers read the future in the pattern of their shells.

The tortoise is a traditional college beast. These shelly creatures live at Balliol, Corpus Christi, Trinity, and Christ Church in the college gardens, and are periodically stumbled upon by students and gardeners. Balliol had a tortoise called Rosa (after the Polish-born revolutionary socialist Rosa Luxemburg) that lived for at least forty-three years. She disappeared in spring 2004. Rosa had competed in, and won many times, the June Tortoise Fair at Corpus Christi, which has been televized.

At the fair the president places competing tortoises in a group at the centre of a ring of lettuces. The first tortoise to reach a succulent leaf is the winner. In 2012, Worcester's 'Zoom' won, beating among others Magdalen's 'Oscar de la Tortoise' and Univ's 'Percy'. The tortoises themselves, excited by the atmosphere and proximity of their own kind, have been more interested in mating (which is initiated with the male tortoise bashing the shell of its mate with its own shell) than in racing. It has been noted that some tortoises are gay. The Corpus tortoises, called Fox and Oldham after the college's founders, live in the president's garden, with winter quarters in the gardener's shed. Trinity is the proud owner of two college tortoises, of which a representative has been present for the past 140 years in the garden.

Figure 14 Owl, pelican, and bees. Sundial base, Corpus Christi College

INSECTS

Warden John Wilkins (1614–72) oversaw the 'Experimental Clubbe' of natural philosophers at Wadham College that was to become the Royal Society at the Restoration. Wilkins was married to Oliver Cromwell's sister, but after the return of the king he became Bishop of Chester, which says something about his political and worldly abilities. Wilkins was said to have had in his garden at Wadham some glass beehives, so that the insects could be observed while doing their work of honey-making. Their internal order could be studied and the honey extracted without destroying the bees.

The statutes of Corpus Christi College, dating to 1517, read: 'We, therefore, Richard Fox, by Divine Providence, Bishop of Winchester, being both desirous ourselves of ascending by this latter to heaven … and being anxious to aid and assist others in a similar ascent and entrance, have founded, reared and constructed in the University of Oxford … a certain bee garden which we have named the College of Corpus Christi, wherein scholars, like ingenious bees are day by day to make wax to the honour of God, and honey, dropping sweetness, to the profit of themselves and of all Christians.' The bees here symbolize hard work.

SEA CREATURES

Lincoln College chapel (built 1629–31) has enamelled windows by Abraham van Linge showing biblical scenes, including the whale vomiting out Jonah. Abraham and his brother Bernard came from Holland. They used vitreous enamels on a 'blank canvas' of glass, which was then fired. Lead lining was also used to keep the different pieces of coloured glass together. The duration and intensity of firing determined the final colour and the type of enamel.

❖

The Headington Shark at 2 New High Street, Headington, was created in 1986 by John Buckley on Bill Heine's house as a protest on Nagasaki Day (9 August) against nuclear weapons and atomic power. He said, 'The shark was to express someone feeling totally impotent, ripping a hole in their roof out of a sense of impotence and anger and desperation.' Some twenty-five feet long, it is made of painted fibreglass. There has been much controversy due to planning laws and damage to

Figure 15 Headington Shark

neighbouring houses. The Department of the Environment finally ruled in 1992 that the shark did not spoil the view and could therefore stay. Bill Heine, a radio presenter and well-known local character, has written a twenty-fifth-anniversary book about the shark and its tail/tale.

❖

The Trout Inn, where Godstow Road crosses the Thames at Wolvercote, is a very popular pub for summer wining and dining. It began as a fisherman's house but was already an inn by 1625. Extensive rebuilding took place in 1737. Inside are an original stone fireplace and a dado of seventeenth-century wood panelling. The floors are lined with stone flags and the rooms are dark, with leaded windows. Outside there is a terrace by the river, where one can soak up the sun and beer while watching the peacocks and (presumably) trout in the water. This inn is mentioned in 'The Scholar Gypsy' by Matthew Arnold. Godstow Bridge is part medieval and part late Victorian. The river flows around an island, over a weir on one side and smoothly down on the other, passing the inn. The local name for a weir and a pool is a lasher.

❖

The Perch Inn is on the north side of Binsey Green. It was built in the seventeenth century and there have been many changes since, not least as a result of the gutting of the pub following a fire that started in the thatched roof, once in 1977 and again more recently.

MYTHICAL BEASTS

The Radcliffe Infirmary merman, or Triton, sat on his fishy tail supporting a shallow dish as a fountain in the forecourt of the old hospital. This fountain was designed in 1857 by John Bell and fabricated in terracotta by J. M. Blashfield of Praed Street, Paddington. Triton is the son of Poseidon, Greek god of the sea. He has the head and torso of a man with the tail of a fish. A new Triton has replaced the old one, which was badly eroded by years of exposure to the elements.

Another rare sea creature to look out for is the ceramic mermaid above Hayman's fish counter in the Covered Market. She smiles down benignly at customers as they buy their red snapper or turbot.

⁂

The founder of St Hilda's Hall (later St Hilda's College), in 1893, was Dorothea Beale, Principal of Cheltenham Ladies' College. The arms of St Hilda's are described in heraldic terms as 'Azure on a fess or between in chief two unicorns heads couped and in base a coiled serpent argent three Estoiles gules'. The Beale family used as their crest a unicorn's head, which, as the college adviser said, 'with its ancient traditions, seemed not inappropriate to a ladies' college'. The unicorn is, of course, a sign of virginity.

In Isidore of Seville's *Etymologiae*, we are told that one thrust of the unicorn's horn may kill an elephant. In the Middle Ages bestiaries taught how a unicorn could

Figure 16 Lion and Unicorn, Sheldonian Theatre

be captured by a maiden. In the Greek *Physiologus* we read, 'How it is captured. A virgin is placed before it and it springs into the virgin's lap and she warms it with love and carries it off to the palace of Kings.'

❖

Confucius, after his visit to the librarian Lao-tzu, said, 'Birds fly, fish swim, animals run. The running animal can be caught in a trap, the swimmer in a net and the flier by an arrow. But there is the dragon; I don't know how it rides on the wind or how it reaches the heavens. Today I met Lao-tzu and I can say that I have seen the dragon.'

The heraldic dragon has a huge body of a reptilian nature, covered with a mail of plate and scales ending in a stinger. From gaping jaws with formidable fangs, he belches flames. He has round luminous eyes, a dangerous spike on his nose, a forked tongue, eagle's feet and bat's wings. The dragon in heraldry is a symbol of power, wisdom, and astuteness.

In 1877 a group of professors, heads of colleges, and clerics who wished to educate their young sons formed a 'visiting council' headed by Dean Liddell. The resulting school was initially in St Giles. The first intake of boys called it 'Dragon School', after St George and the dragon on the coinage of the day and also after the Reverend H. B. George, who was on the council. Caps and badges had a dragon symbol and the boys were known as 'the dragons' to their peers. However, it was not until 1921 that it officially became the Dragon School.

On the corner with St Michael's Street is No. 37 Cornmarket (Northgate House), which was built around 1860. At first-floor level is a splendid early electricity bracket in cast iron ending in a dragon's head that is spitting fire over the shoppers below. It is currently painted black but surely gold would be more appropriate. He dates from around 1895 and was spared when Cornmarket was relit in 1974–5.

❖

If the lion is the king of the beasts and the eagle the king of the birds, the griffin (or gryphon) is the legendary creature that combines the two, having the body of a lion and the head, wings, and talons of an eagle. With prominent ears like those of a horse, griffins are renowned for their ability to protect and guard, and are often shown as the guardians of treasure. In heraldic terms they signify courage and boldness, intelligence and strength.

In the Middle Ages a griffin was used an emblem of Christ. According to Isidore of Seville in his *Etymologiae*: 'Christ is a lion because he reigns and has great strength, and an eagle because, after the resurrection, he ascended to heaven.'

⁂

Dragons and griffins are two heraldic beasts associated with Trinity College, both of which came to the college courtesy of its founder, Sir Thomas Pope. It uses Pope's coat of arms of three gryphons (this is the college's preferred spelling), otherwise known as griffins, 'per pale or and azure on a chevron between three gryphons' heads erased four fleurs-de-lys all counter charged'. Pope's personal crest was a double-headed dragon: 'Two dragons' heads endorsed erased, a coronet about their necks counter charged or and azure, set on a wreath or and vert.' This was on Pope's seal and is on some college seals too.

Figure 17 Gryphon bookstand, Trinity College

Both gryphons and dragons appear in different parts of the college: for example, carved in panelling, over the college gate, and in china and tablemats. The old college barge had a dragon figurehead and Trinity has had a debating society called The Gryphon on and off since the 1880s. There has always been a great deal of confusion as to which beasts are dragons and which are gryphons. For instance, there is an eighteenth-century lectern which is carved in the shape of a dragon but is known as 'the gryphon'. Dragons are related to snakes and so have forked tongues and scales, while gryphons are partly birds and have feathers and beaks, but the distinction remains confusing.

❖

No. 65 Holywell Street has two grotesque carved brackets, one a head with breasts beneath and the other a dragonish head with a beaky nose and pointed ears. They were probably rescued from the original building and are dated A.S. and C.S. 1639. The house itself is nineteenth-century.

On a west-facing wall on the Bodleian Library, tucked in behind the Sheldonian Theatre, are nine grotesques. They don't have a waterspout like gargoyles, but are carved in fantastic shapes. These grotesques were designed in 2007 by nine Oxfordshire schoolchildren, aged between eleven and fourteen and were carved in stone by a local stonemason, Alec Peever, and his wife, Fiona. The grotesques are a dodo; a green man; three men in a boat (from the book of that name by Jerome K. Jerome); Tweedledum and Tweedledee (from Lewis Carroll's *Through the Looking-Glass*); the boar from the Queen's College legend; Thomas Bodley, the founder of the Bodleian Library; Aslan, the lion from C. S. Lewis's Narnia books; General Pitt Rivers, founder of the Pitt Rivers Museum; and a beast from J. R. R. Tolkien's *Lord of the Rings* books. They are very fine carvings and will look out from the Bodleian for many years to come.

From Queen's Lane, one can see a row of stone carvings on the southern side of New College, where grotesque human faces alternate with some fascinating animal carvings. In addition to native creatures, such as beetles, otters, and a pair of dormice nest-building among sheafs of wheat, there are more exotic animals, such as a bush-baby, an emu, and a mongoose entwined with a cobra.

LITERARY CREATURES

As everyone knows, Christ Church is the college of Charles Dodgson, or Lewis Carroll, who as a mathematics don taught here and made friends with Alice Liddell and her sisters. *Alice's Adventures in Wonderland* and *Through the Looking-Glass* contain some of the most memorable animal creations in literature. These include the White Rabbit, the Cheshire Cat, the March Hare, the Mouse, the Dodo, the Caterpillar, the Lory, the Eaglet, the Dormouse, the Gryphon, and the Mock Turtle.

The Mock Turtle sings 'Soo-oop of the e-e-evening / Beautiful, beautiful soup'. Christ Church was indeed known for its turtle soup. The live turtles were kept in the 'Mercury' pond in Tom Quad, where the college children could ride on their backs. There are a couple of shells hanging up in the kitchen and they are some two to three feet across.

The beautiful illustrations by John Tenniel were a major selling point in the original edition of *Alice*. Tenniel had a long association with *Punch* magazine, for which he drew political and social cartoons. Many of Tenniel's drawings show similarities to the drawings Dodgson did for his manuscript 'Alice's Adventures Underground'. The animals in Tenniel's drawings are much more lifelike and realistic than Dodgson's cruder efforts, but in many cases Tenniel has adopted Dodgson's original vision. Tenniel had spent several years at the London Zoological Gardens, drawing animals for his Aesop's Fables (1848). The Alice animals all look very realistic. Dodgson may have used Thomas Bewick's *General History of Quadrupeds* (1790) as a guide, and Tenniel almost certainly did.

In the opinion of the Christ Church librarians, the Alice animals are not based on specific people from the college or from Oxford, but we do know that the Lory was Lorina Liddell, the Eaglet was Edith Liddell and that Alice was herself. Dodgson's imagination was so great that although he must have borrowed, like all authors, from real life, his inventions are mostly brilliantly original. The Dodo was Dodgson with his stammer, and his friend Duckworth was the Duck, while Dinah the cat was Alice's own pet.

❖

C. S. Lewis's Narnia books are famously full of animals that are larger than their equivalents in this world. Aslan the lion, who is the son of God, is the best known. I loved these books as a child and it seemed to me only natural that animals could talk and have characters. The books also include mythological beasts, such as winged horses and dragons. It seemed an entire world to me and one that was in some ways better than reality.

⁕

J. R. R. Tolkien's animals are much darker than Lewis's. From the dragon Smaug in *The Hobbit* and the ghostly riders, the Ringwraiths, in *The Lord of the Rings*, these are creatures that belong to a much less cosy world than Narnia and they come out of the author's experiences as a soldier in the First World War, in the trenches.

⁕

Philip Pullman's 'His Dark Materials' trilogy creates a world where each human character has a shape-shifting 'daemon' or personal animal companion and soulmate. The wicked Mrs Coulter tries to separate children from their animal spirit and thus destroy the child's joy in life. The heroine Lara's daemon is called Pantalaimon and can change shape but is usually a pine marten. Philip Pullman based Jordan College in the books on Exeter College.

A CONGREGATION OF OTHER ANIMALS

The large area of land bounded by Wolvercote village, the railway and the canal, Botley Road and the River Thames has been used as grazing land for cattle, horses, and geese since before King Alfred gave it to the Freemen of Oxford in the tenth century. The earliest evidence of occupation of Port Meadow comes from Bronze Age burial mounds, and the Iron Age dwellings that have been found show that beasts grazed there also at that time. King Alfred's Freemen won grazing rights because they had helped him fight the marauding Danes. By virtue of the grazing rights, both Port Meadow and Wolvercote Common have been saved from development of any kind and are sometimes referred to as 'England's oldest monument'. Both are mentioned in the Domesday Book of 1086. Earthworks from the English Civil War can be seen in the southern section. During the seventeenth and eighteenth centuries horse racing was a popular sport and in the twentieth century early aircraft landed on the meadow.

Looking at the meadow on a sunny day and watching the cattle and horses move slowly across the landscape as they crop the turf, there is a great feeling of continuity over time and season. This continuity of grazing has produced a unique flora which includes bird's-foot trefoil, tall thistles, yarrow, and rest harrow. These are found in the dry, gravelly soil of the northern section and are referred to as limestone grassland. The southern section is flooded very often by the Thames and wetland species such as arrow grass, strawberry clover, and the very rare creeping marsh wort grow there. The annual winter floods bring thousands of birds to Port Meadow – lapwing, plover, teal, widgeon, and Canada geese are all there. Waders and freshwater fowl, gulls, terns, and songbirds complete this wonderful scene.

On the Broad Street and Parks Road sides of the Weston Library are coats of arms, carved in stone, with animal supporters (see back cover). Gryphons (Earl Halifax), elephant and beaver (Oxford City), deer (Duke of Gloucester), and ducks (Thomas Brassey) are some of the animals shown here.

Iffley Parish Church dates from the twelfth century, with a thirteenth-century extension to the chancel. The twelfth-century church was built of Oxfordshire stone by Robert de St Remi between 1175 and 1182. The chancel was extended eastward in the middle of the thirteenth century. The Romanesque style shows most clearly in the west door surrounds and on a smaller scale at the south door. The south door is carved with rosettes on the innermost border, with leaf designs, beasts and monsters, including a lion, a sphinx, a merman, and a bird. Outside this is a curve of very alien-looking beaked heads wedged together. The capitals of the flanking columns are carved with fighting men, Samson and the lion, centaurs and beasts, and a lion attacking a horse. The west door has four rows of chevrons surrounded by two rows of beak-heads. Outside this is a series of richly carved cartouches joined by lion's heads. They are an eagle (probably for

St John); Aquarius; Pisces; a winged bull (St Luke); a winged figure (angel of St Matthew); a dove; a monster or Jonah's whale; a dove and a scroll; a winged lion (St Mark); a winged ox; an eagle; a seraph; and monsters. Badly weathered monsters begin and end this sequence. This is a really fine piece of work which has suffered somewhat from the prevailing weather, but the vividness of the carving can still be fairly appreciated.

The first window in the south wall of the nave is filled by a stained-glass piece designed by John Piper (1903–92) and given to Iffley Church by his widow, Myfanwy, in 1995. It was made by David Wasley. It shows the Tree of Life and the animals at the Nativity or at the Passion, who cry:

Cock: *Christus natus est* [Christ is born].
Goose: *Quando? Quando?* [When? When?]
Crow: *In haec nocte* [On this night].
Owl: *Ubi? Ubi?* [Where? Where?]
Lamb: *Bethlehem! Bethlehem!*

The legend was that the animals spoke at the birth of Christ and that the Tree

Figure 18 The Piper window, St Mary's Church, Iffley

of Life 'yielded twelve crops of fruit, one for each month of the year. The leaves of the trees serve for the healing of nations, and every accursed thing shall disappear' (Book of Revelation).

In an interpretation of the Passion, the cock can be seen as Peter denying Christ, the crow as human suffering and frailty, the goose as human foolishness, and the owl as wisdom. The lamb, then, is Christ, who provides an answer to all the beasts. Whatever the interpretation, the window shines with jewelled colours.

✥

St Peter-in-the-East Church (now St Edmund Hall Library) has a very interesting twelfth-century crypt, with five east–west and three north–south bays. It has vaults with plain cross-arches between the bays, supported by cylindrical columns with scalloped capitals. A third capital shows foliage, beasts, a winged monster, and a scene of two men and a beast, possibly Daniel and the lion.

✥

The house at No. 62 Banbury Road, built in 1864–5 by E. G. Bruton, has a steep tympanum or pointed panel above the doorway carved with foliage, a seated king, a

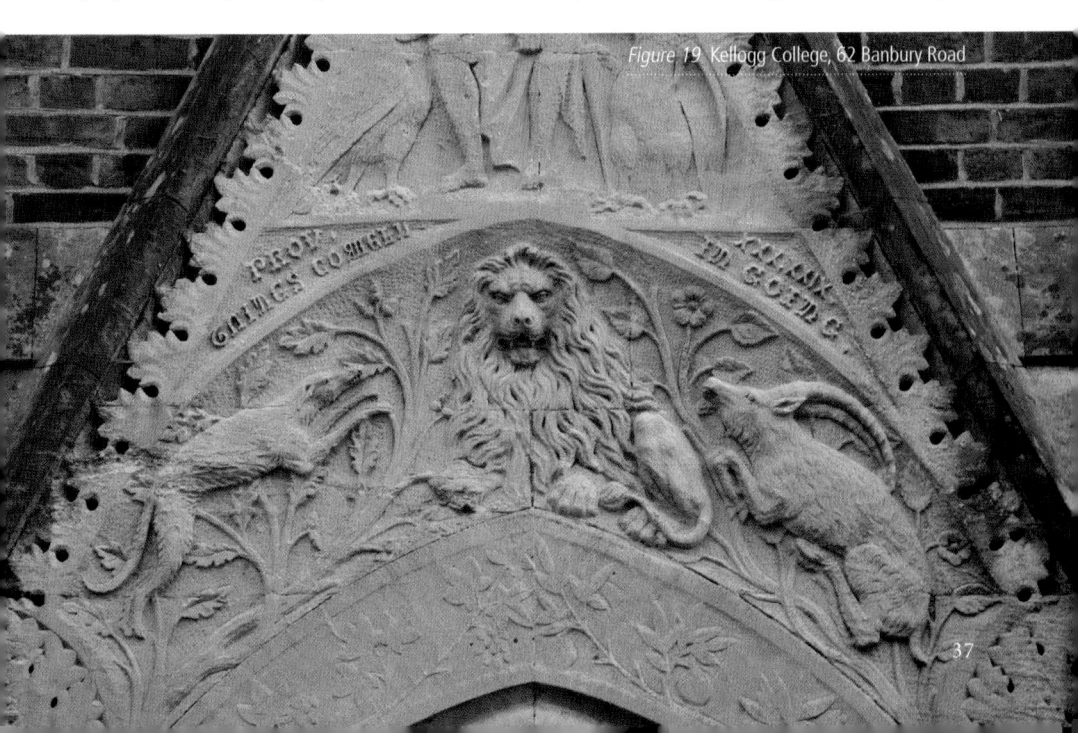

Figure 19. Kellogg College, 62 Banbury Road

lion, a Capricorn, a greyhound, and two birds. The house was built for the Reverend R. St John Tyrwhitt of Christ Church, artist, author, and disciple of Ruskin, who did decorative work at the Oxford Museum of Natural History. The carving was by Hungerford Pollen. The building now forms part of Kellogg College.

❖

The Examination Schools, designed by T. G. Jackson, are sumptuous High Victorian, Jacobean-style rooms for the undergraduates to take their exams in. Their results are also displayed here. The floor of the Great Hall, which is in coloured marbles, includes mosaics showing animals from Aesop's Fables such as the tortoise and the hare. This building is not well known and is not usually open to the public.

❖

The beautiful and symbolic carving above the entrance to Merton College contains many elements of the New Testament, including animals, birds, and trees. It is a history of St John the Baptist, who stands at the right of the scene, holding a book. He is telling of the coming of Christ. To his left is the founder of Merton, the Bishop of Rochester, who is kneeling in prayer. Next is a unicorn, symbolic of Christ's incarnation and exaltation. In the centre of the carving is a large book, mentioned in the Book of Revelation by St John, which is called the Book of Seven Seals. This represents the Day of Judgement. The lion, which is

Figure 20 Frieze, Merton College

looking at the book, stands for the resurrection of Christ, and to its left is the Lamb of God with the sun of righteousness shining upon it. The charming rabbits in their burrows run across the bottom of the scene, with two hunting dogs keeping them in check as they scamper about like wayward humans. In the trees behind are two eagles (the emblems of St John) and above The Book of Seven Seals in the ash tree (the world tree) is the pelican, which piously feeds its young with its own blood, obtained by plucking at its breast.

The trees are, from the left, pomegranate, apple, orange, ash, box or hornbeam, oak, beech or sallow, walnut or myrtle, and poplar. These trees also have Christian meanings. In the order above: eternal life, the tree of knowledge, fecundity, world tree, fidelity, the church, palm leaves, Christ's body, the walnut shell shielding his divine nature and humanity.

The symbolism of carvings such as these told a story to the illiterate populace of medieval Oxford, who knew all of the connections that birds and animals had, not only in the Bible but also in the Life of Christ. The historian Anthony à Wood, who lived across the street from Merton, said that the History of St John had been damaged in Oliver Cromwell's time but that it had been 'repaired and now styled over in white colours' in 1682.

Also at Merton, the Fitzjames Arch shelters the signs of the zodiac, including a really vicious-looking Scorpio.

✣

Figure 21 Roof boss of Scorpio, Merton College

The two most notable examples of wooden misericords showing beasts and human forms are at All Souls College Chapel, where they date from the mid fifteenth century, and at New College, where they were carved in the late fourteenth century. The extreme liveliness of the carvings reflects the spirits of the medieval craftsmen who made them. Building churches in the Middle Ages was for the glory of God, but the humanity of their creators show in these exuberant carvings. A lovely owl, sheep, a griffin, a dragon, and a goat monster at All Souls; a double-bodied lion's head, a peacock, monsters, hawks, and a swan at New College.

Meanwhile, at Christ Church, in the presbytery choir stalls, are some fabulous beasts in highly polished, chestnut-coloured wooden bench ends.

❖

The Chequers, at 131a High Street, was a private house from 1260 to 1434. In 1460 it was a moneylender's premises, using the Roman sign, the chequerboard. In the early sixteenth century it became the home of Alderman Richard Kent, and was known as Kent's Hall. It was granted its first licence as an inn the following century. In 1757 it was displaying a camel from Cairo; in 1758 Siamese twins from Witney; and by 1762 there were fourteen large animals, including a 'sea lioness', another camel, an American marsupial (it's unclear what this could have been), a racoon, and a very large fish (possibly a shark). Richard Kent's original building still forms the basis of the inn today.

❖

The Red Barn, a building with high, seventy-foot-long walls, was built to house Charles Peel's big game museum at No. 12 Woodstock Road. The taxidermists in Victorian times must have worked overtime, because the collection included a number of African species shot by Peel and also a polar bear. The chief attraction was a giraffe called Gerald, as well as a hippo and elephants. Peel opened the museum in 1906 but it lasted only five years before he moved to Exeter. The building went on to become the first Oxford Playhouse and there is a blue plaque commemorating both institutions. The Bodleian Library has a 1906 catalogue of the big game museum.

❖

AN OXFORD BESTIARY

The delightful Worcester College Chapel was designed by James Wyatt (1746–1813) in the classical style. Its ionic columns and pilasters are original, but the rest of the chapel was completely redecorated in 1864–6 in the High Victorian style by the architect William Burges (1827–81). Burges also worked at Cardiff Castle and Castell Coch in Wales and Harrow School. At the end of each pew are beautiful carved animals in the most lively style. They are made of teak and are one of the lesser-known sights of Oxford.

Figure 22 Elephant bench end, Worcester College Chapel

AN OXFORD BESTIARY

The animals are arranged thus:

East Window

hippo	owl		cock	tapir
walrus	lizard	snake	unicorn	whale
	anteater	rhino	pelican	eagle
	bear	kangaroo	feline	horse
	swan	hyena	elephant	crocodile
	emu	boar	dog	pangolin
	tortoise	camel	lion	lamb
	tiger	buffalo		

and by the organ seat there are two grinning felines.

Some of the animals have biblical associations, but others are there for their beauty and liveliness alone.

❖

Figure 23 Camel bench end, Worcester College Chapel

42

AN OXFORD BESTIARY

Nineteenth-century Oxford was full of eccentrics. The theologian and geologist William Buckland (1784–1856) was born near Axminster and used to find fossil shells in the River Axe and on the seashore near Lyme Regis. He graduated from Corpus Christi College, Oxford, in 1804 and became a don there, before becoming a reader in geology in 1818. In 1825 he became the Vicar of Islip and was a canon at Christ Church. He was famous for trying to eat at least one of every species of animal he could lay his hands on. Christ Church had its own Anatomy School until the middle of the nineteenth century and lots of specimens were eventually removed to the Oxford University Museum when it opened in 1860. The specimens included a baby elephant, a tuna fish, and a giraffe. The giraffe had a plaster tail because some local dogs had made off with the real one when it was being prepared for taxidermy.

A famous print shows Buckland holding a large ammonite and lecturing to a recognizable audience of University worthies. The lecture took place in the Old

Figure 24 William Buckland lecturing, Old Ashmolean

Ashmolean Museum, surrounded by mammoth tusks, fossils, and ichthyosaurus bones, on 15 February 1823. Behind Buckland is the tiny figure of Charles Daubeny, who was notoriously short in stature and known as 'Little Dubs'. Buckland was an elegant and witty person who took geology seriously, but not geologists. His generation, including Charles Lyell, inspired Charles Darwin, whose ideas swept away the Creationist creed of theology and changed the world.

William's son Frank was a naturalist. In the *Life of Frank Buckland* by George C. Bompas we are told that in June 1834, 'a live turtle was sent down from London, to be dressed for the banquet in Christ Church Hall. My father tied a long rope around the turtle's fin and let him have a swim in "Mercury", the ornamental water in the middle of Christ Church quad, while I held the string. I recollect too, that my father made me stand on the back of the turtle while he held me on (I was then a little fellow) and I had a ride for a few yards as it swam round and round the pond.'

Bompas also records: 'In his early home at Christ Church, besides the stuffed creatures that shared the hall with the rocking horse, there were cages full of snakes, and of green frogs, in the dining room where the sideboard groaned under successive layers of fossils, and the candles stood on the ichthyosauri's vertebrae. Guinea pigs were often running over the table; and occasionally the pony, having trotted down the steps from the garden, would push open the dining room door and career round the table with three laughing children on his back, and then, marching through the front door, and down the steps, would continue his course around Tom Quad.

'In the stable yard and large wood-house were the fox, rabbits, guinea pigs and ferrets, hawks and owls, the magpie and jackdaw, besides dogs, cats and poultry, and in the garden was the tortoise (on whose back the children would stand to try its strength), and toads immured in various pots, to test the truth of their supposed life in rock cells.

'There were visits also to the Clarendon, where Dr Buckland was forming the nucleus of the present Geological Museum of Oxford, and to the Old Ashmolean Museum. Here the children might ride a stuffed zebra and knew the animals as friends, if not yet as relations.

AN OXFORD BESTIARY

'In October 1844 Frank entered Christ Church as a commoner. There was a court between Fell's Buildings, where he had his room on the ground floor, and the Canons' gardens where he housed his collection of zoological and anatomical specimens, living and dead. Among the former were a young bear named Tiglath Pileser, Jacko the monkey, an eagle, a jackal, marmots, guinea pigs, squirrels, dormice, an adder, harmless snakes and glow worms, tortoises, green frogs, and a chameleon. Skeletons and stuffed specimens were numerous, and often anatomical preparations were in progress in the court. The live pets had a tendency to stray. One morning Frank was called in haste to remove a marmot from the chapter house. Another morning the eagle stationed himself in the chapel doorway and attacked those who wished to enter, till he was rolled up in one of the student's gowns and carried off ignominiously. Some of the pets also had an unfortunate tendency to eat each other.

'Tiglath Pileser, named after the Assyrian king, was about six months old when he entered Christ Church, where he lived in a corner of the court. He was provided with a cap and gown, and in this costume was taken to wine parties, or went boating with his master. Tig, as he was familiarly called, took part in the proceedings of the British Association at Oxford in 1847, attending in cap and gown the garden party at the Botanic Garden and receiving a visit from Mr Moncton Milnes, who attempted to mesmerize him in his corner. This made the bear furious, but he gradually yielded to the influence and at last fell senseless to the ground.'

⁕

The Ashmolean Museum houses both art and archaeological finds. The gallery of Minoan art, mostly from Knossos, includes some very beautiful seal stones that depict animals: for example, a boar, a sheep, a man jumping over a bull, a dog barking at a goat, a wild goat, a butterfly, water fowl, a deer hit by a spear, a cat seizing a swan, a flying bird and two calves, and a tree. These are all carved on different gemstones and are a delight to behold.

In the next gallery are two stone lions from Golgoi in Cyprus, and red-figure vessels of various kinds showing a hound chasing a hare, Heracles wrestling the

AN OXFORD BESTIARY

Nemean lion on a sixth-century BC amphora, and a Laconian hound on a red-figure cup of the fifth-century BC. There are many examples of animals in Greek art; they all show not only a love of and devotion to beasts but also that animals were a very important part of the culture and psychology of ancient peoples.

In the art collection of the Ashmolean is a rare portrait (1650–80) of an ordinary dog by an unknown Genoese artist. The dog is lying on a chipped stone step – he is not an aristocratic hound. He has brown fur with white tips and his mouth is slightly open, showing his tongue. He is looking both sleepy and alert at the same time. It is a portrait full of character. At any moment, the viewer feels, that dog could get up and start investigating his surroundings.

Figure 25 Portrait of a dog, Ashmolean Museum

In the eighteenth-century gallery is a portrait of a young woman with a macaw by Giovanni Battista Tiepolo (1696–1770), the gentleness of the girl contrasting with the fierceness of the parrot.

In the new Egyptian galleries there is a splendid stone Ram of Amun from about 680 BC, with a small statuette of Taharqa between his front legs. The ram is life-size, with an inscription saying that Taharqa is the son of Amun. There is also a magnificent lion with a stylized mane in red pottery that would have guarded a building's entrance.

Canopic jars which contained entrails can be seen. They have the heads of falcons, monkeys, or cats as lids.

In the Chinese galleries are a glazed terracotta horse and camel. From the Silk Road is a golden bull, approximately four centimetres long, which is lying down, and from the Caspian region a wonderfully shaped humpbacked pottery bull dating from about 1200–1000 BC.

Figure 26 Minoan jar with octopus, Ashmolean Museum

A striking octopus jar dating from 1450–1400 BC that was given by the Greek government to the Ashmolean is at the centre of the Minoan gallery.

In the gallery filled mostly with still-life paintings is a picture of a mallard male duck and pale-brown female preening their feathers. This charming portrait is by Johannes Spruyt (1627–71).

There are two particularly fine early Renaissance paintings here, *The Hunt in the Forest* by Paolo Uccello and *The Forest Fire* by Piero di Cosimo. The former was painted as an imaginary, idealized scene in which the crescent moon links with Diana, Goddess of the Chase. It is an allegory. Hunting was seen as the game of life, as in love or war, where the stag was a noble beast; or as in the pursuit of salvation. Poems about hunting or falconry were popular and *The Hunt* would have been viewed in an important room at shoulder height, so the lessons of the scene could be seen by the entire household.

The Forest Fire is also an allegory. The animals and birds fleeing the forest are beautifully realized by Piero. It is thought that the scene refers to *De Rerum Natura* (On the Nature of the Universe) by Lucretius, a Roman philosopher and poet. He writes of man's evolution from living wild in the forest to being able to use fire and become more civilized. In *The Forest Fire* we see a huntsman and animals bellowing, shouting, and calling in their fear of the fire. Lucretius discusses the development of language, from brutish calls and birds' cries to man's speech. He talks of the fire melting rocks to produce gold, silver, tin, and lead for man to learn to use. These themes of language and society changed through the use of fire are shown in the primitiveness of fire in the forest, and the depiction of the language animals and man use to survive. The civilization of the huntsman contrasts with the primeval nature of the forest. The satyrs' heads painted on pigs and deer were a last-minute joke on Piero's part, designed to please his patron. Piero's imagination and love of nature must have been fired by the observations made by Lucretius in his work.

❖

The old Indian Institute on the corner of Holywell and Catte Street is a Mitton stone building with delightful details that show its original use. At first-floor level there is a stone frieze of four animal heads – an elephant, a lion, a buffalo, and a growling tiger. At the second-floor level is a stone frieze of Hindu demi-gods. They are beautifully sculpted by William Aimonier and bring a really individual nature to this Victorian building. High up on a cupola is a charming elephant weather-vane in gold. This beast (with a howdah on its back) has a view, envied by many a tourist, up Broad Street and of the Bodleian, Sheldonian, and Clarendon Buildings. The Institute was designed by Basil Champneys in 1883–5.

Figure 27 Indian Institute, Broad Street

Sir Monier Monier-Williams, Professor of Sanskrit, hoped to found a place where India could be studied by Europeans and the West could be studied by Indians. In 1968 the collection and archive were moved to the New Bodleian when (against many people's wishes) the Institute became the History Faculty Library. The archive at the Bodleian is the largest collection of writings on India in Europe.

❖

Outside the front door of the Oxford University Museum of Natural History is a stone carved with animals, birds, and fish to commemorate the 150th anniversary of the Great Debate in 1860 between Samuel Wilberforce, Bishop of Oxford, and Thomas Henry Huxley, known as 'Darwin's Bulldog'. Wilberforce spoke against Charles Darwin's ideas on evolution as put forward in *On the Origin of Species*, which directly countered the story told in Genesis in the Bible. The Bishop asked if Huxley was descended from an ape, to which Huxley replied that he would rather be descended from an ape than from a bishop who used his intelligence to rubbish serious scientific discussion. Lady Brewster fainted on hearing these impious remarks. The room where this heated debate took place is on the first floor, left of the main entrance, and now contains a collection of beetles. The museum was conceived as a way of modernizing science in Oxford in 1850. The University lagged a long way behind London and Cambridge, concentrating too much on classics and theology. Charles Daubeny, Professor of Chemistry

AN OXFORD BESTIARY

Figure 28 Henry Acland with his pet monkey

and Botany, and Henry Acland, a Reader in Anatomy, argued that physics, chemistry, and physiology should be taught to students. Eventually the university agreed to build a museum to house its natural history collections, at a cost of £40,000. It was built in five years and opened in 1860. The British Association for the Advancement of Science met in June 1860, and the clash between Wilberforce and Huxley took place on the last day of that month.

The whole building reflects nature, both plant and animal life. The cast-iron columns are crowned with metal leaves and flowers. The wonderful capitals of the stone columns around the central courtyard were carved with frogs, birds, mice, snakes, butterflies etc. by the O'Shea brothers (from Ireland) in such a lively, naturalistic way that they seem as fresh as ever 150 years later. They used bunches of flowers brought from the Botanic Garden as their models.

Charles Darwin's ideas had come from earlier naturalists. The collection of dinosaur and human bones gathered by William Buckland was put on display in the new museum. Buckland gave public lectures on fossils from 1813 and he attracted a lot of publicity for the bones of what he called a 'Megalosaurus' ('big lizard') that had been found in a slate mine in Stonesfield, Oxfordshire. Clearly these bones could not fit into a world that, according to Bishop Ussher, had been created in 4004 BC. Buckland also exhibited his 'Red Lady', found when he was digging a cave in the Gower Peninsula in 1823. The skeleton was covered with red ochre and had shell ornaments. It is now known to be the skeleton of a man in his early twenties dating to 29,000 years ago (before the last Ice Age) and is the oldest skeleton of modern man ever found in this country.

The collections of animal, insect, and marine life add up to half a million specimens. Some of these are Darwin's, collected on the voyage of the *Beagle*: for example, crabs and tortoises. Others, like the dodo's skin and bones, are almost unique.

Also important are the Hope Entomological Collections. The Reverend Frederick Hope left his entire collection of insects to Oxford University in 1849. Much extended since then, the collection now houses over 5 million specimens, including many rare and wonderful beetles. J. B. S. Haldane famously remarked that God must be inordinately fond of beetles to have created so many different species.

The articulated skeletons of animals are a feature of the main gallery as are many stuffed specimens.

The Great Debate Plinth is situated on the grass directly outside the entrance to the museum. It was designed in 2009 by an Oxfordshire schoolgirl, Poppy Simonson, on the theme of *On the Origin of Species*, and has Darwin's finches, fish, and a marine iguana from the Galapagos, all carved by Alec Peever.

The museum's tower has vents in it and in the years after the last war

Figure 29 Plinth outside the University Museum of Natural History

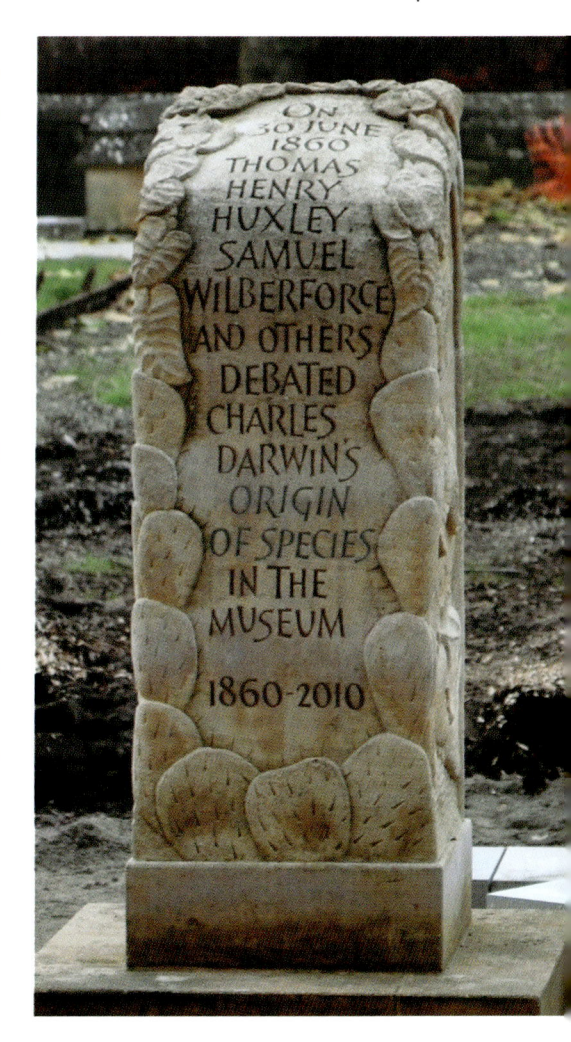

AN OXFORD BESTIARY

Andrew Lack studied the migratory swifts that used the tower to nest in. They got in by way of the vents. Lack and his researchers had to climb a very long ladder to get into the tower roof space, but once there they studied the breeding swifts, their chicks and the parasites they hosted. The work was written up in a book called *Swifts in a Tower*, which is now out of print but is available on the internet.

Other museum residents include the bee colony on the south stairs. The bees would forage in the surrounding area and come back with pollen to the window containing the combs in a glass case, so that they could be observed. Watching bees is a very ancient pastime: Pliny the Elder (AD 23–79) has a chapter devoted to bees in his *Natural History*.

❖

The ethnographic collections of Oxford University are housed in the Pitt Rivers Museum, the entrance to which is at the back of the Museum of Natural History. Beyond its recently renovated entrance, a spacious hall opens out in front of visitors, in which children with flashing torches explore the displays. At the far end is an enormous totem pole carved by Haida artists from a cedar tree. Among the animals represented are a bear eating a frog, a bear with two cubs, and a raven holding a human between its wings. The pole was made to mark the adoption of a daughter and the figures are ancestral crests of the adopted girl's, new family. There are lots of other animals in the museum such as a painted wooden figure of a rhinoceros hornbill from

Figure 30 Haida totem pole, Pitt Rivers Museum

Sarawak, made as a symbol of war in the days when headhunting was still practised. There is a brass Indian peacock, a buffalo mask from Cameroon symbolizing courage, power, and strength, and a horse-headed fiddle from Mongolia. Familiar domestic animals like the cat were sacred in ancient Egypt to the goddess Bast and there is a bronze one here. An owl from Japan looks out from its case with beady eyes. Throughout human history, animals and birds, fish and insects have been at the very centre of life, from providing food, at the most mundane level, to being represented in everyday objects, religious practices, and art. The Pitt Rivers displays illustrate a great range of animal influences, both cultural and practical.

❖

The Oxford dodo is a rare bird indeed. It came from the collection of the botanist and gardener John Tradescant the Younger (1608–62) and was part of his 'cabinet of curiosities', assembled from all over the world. In the catalogue the stuffed dodo was described as being 'from the island Mauritius; it is not able to fly being so big', and it truly does look ridiculous in a contemporary portrait with a bulging breast, huge beak, and tiny wings. Dodos were eaten by Dutch sailors who landed on the island. They also brought with them pests such as rats and cats, not to mention diseases, all of which finished off the dodo in quick order.

After John Trandescant's death, his stuffed dodo came to Oxford in 1683. Tradescant had left his 'curiosities' to Elias Ashmole, who persuaded the University authorities to build a purpose-made home for them. This is the Old Ashmolean Museum, now the Museum of the History of Science.

And so the dodo remained in Broad Street for just over seventy years. In 1755 the museum authorities sorted out and burned specimens that were rather the worse for wear. This included the stuffed dodo, but the skull with skin and one foot were saved at the last moment, carefully catalogued and kept. In 1860 the remains were moved to the Oxford University Museum, and it was here that Charles Dodgson saw the dodo with Alice, Lorina, and Edith Liddell. His stories about animals became *Alice's Adventures in Wonderland*, in which the dodo organizes a 'caucus race' that all contestants can win, runing for as long or as far as they want.

Figure 31 Dodo, University Museum of Natural History

DNA research suggests that the dodo was related to the pigeon and was more slimline than the bird depicted in the 1650s.

⁜

The synagogue in Richmond Road has a stained-glass window by the Belgian-born Oxford artist Vital Peeters depicting all the animals of the Ark. It seems appropriate to end our book with some words from the Bible that herald the return of these creatures to the land:

> Also he [Noah] sent forth a dove from him, to see if the waters were abated from off the face of the ground. But the dove found no rest for the sole of her foot, and she returned unto him into the ark; for the waters were on the face of the whole earth: then he put forth his hand, and took her, and pulled her in unto him into the ark. And he stayed yet other seven days; and again he sent forth the dove out of the ark. And the dove came in to him in the evening; and lo, in her mouth was an olive leaf plucked off: so Noah knew that the waters were abated from the earth.
> —Genesis 8:8–11

ACKNOWLEDGEMENTS

The author is indebted to the following people and institutions for their assistance in the writing of this booklet: Geoff Ager; The Ashmolean Museum, University of Oxford; Dr Norma Aubertin Potter; Elizabeth Boardman; Jeremy Coote; Judith Curthoys; Dr Robin Darwall-Smith; Emily Downing; Georgina Edwards; Paul Freestone; Clare Hopkins; Amanda Ingram; Chris Jeens; Jacqui Julier; Lesley Levene; Peter Lewis; Janet McMullin; Eddie Mizzi; Rozzi Nicholson-Lailey; Keith Owen; Oxford City Council; Pitt Rivers Museum, University of Oxford; Julian Reid; Michael Riordan; Rachel Robinson; Anna Sander; The President and Fellows of Corpus Christi College, Oxford; The President and Fellows of Trinity College, Oxford; The Principal and Fellows of St Edmund Hall; The Provost and Fellows of Worcester College, Oxford; University Museum of Natural History, University of Oxford; The Warden and Fellows of Merton College, Oxford.

The index was compiled by Dianne Hosmer.

The Greening Lamborn Trust

The author and publisher are grateful to the Greening Lamborn Trust for a generous grant towards the publication of this booklet. The Trust's objective is to promote public interest in the history, architecture, old photographs, and heraldry of Oxford and its neighbourhood by supporting publications and other media that create access to them.

BIBLIOGRAPHY

de Hamel, Christopher, *Book of Beasts*, A Facsimile Copy of MS Bodley 764, Bodleian Library, 2008.

Gunther, R. T., *Oxford Gardens*, Parker & Sons, 1912.

Hibbert, Christopher, and Hibbert, Edward, *The Encyclopedia of Oxford*, Macmillan, 1988.

Honey, Alison, *Ashmolean Floor by Floor*, Ashmolean Museum, 2011.

Morris, Jan, *Oxford*, Oxford University Press, 1978

Newlyn, Lucy, *Chatter of Choughs*, Signal Books, 2001.

Pevsner, Nikolaus, and Sherwood, Jennifer, *Oxfordshire*, Yale University Press, 2002.

Pickering, Jane, *The Oxford Dodo*, Oxford University Museum of Natural History, 2010.

Rohde, E. S., *Oxford's College Gardens*, Herbert Jenkins, 1932.

Royal Commission on Historical Monuments, England, *City of Oxford*, HMSO, 1939.

Whistler, Catherine, *Paulo Uccello's The Hunt in the Forest*, Ashmolean Museum, 2001.

Whistler, Catherine, and Bomford, David, *The Forest Fire by Piero di Cosimo*, Ashmolean Museum, 1999.

AN OXFORD BESTIARY

PICTURE CREDITS

Figure 6: Courtesy of the Principal and Fellows of St Edmund Hall, Oxford.

Figures 9, 12, 13, 14: Courtesy of the President and Fellows of Corpus Christi College, Oxford.

Figure 17: Courtesy of the President and Fellows of Trinity College, Oxford.

Figure 20: Courtesy of the Warden and Fellows of Merton College, Oxford.

Figures 21, 22: Courtesy of the Provost and Fellows of Worcester College, Oxford.

Figures 24, 25: Courtesy of the Ashmolean Museum, University of Oxford.

Figures 28, 30: Courtesy of the University Museum of Natural History, University of Oxford.

Figure 29: Courtesy of the Pitt Rivers Museum, University of Oxford.

INDEX

Page numbers in **bold** indicate illustrations.

Acland, Henry 50, **50**
Aesop's Fables 1, 33, 38
Alfred, King 17, 34
Alice (fictional character) 1, 33
All Souls College 20–3, 40
Angel and Greyhound, The (pub) 8
Ashmole, Elias 53
Ashmolean Museum 1, 10, 12, 14, 45–8
    Minoan jar 47, **47**
    paintings **46**, 47–8
    see also Old Ashmolean Museum

Balliol College 5, **5**, 19, 25
Bear Inn 12, **12**
bears **12**, 40, 42, 45, 52, **52**
Beaumont Palace 7
beavers 4, 35
bees 26, **26**, 26–7, 52
beetles 32, 49, 51
bestiaries 1–2, 15, 29–30
Blackbird, The (pub) **16**, 17
Blackbird Leys 17
Blue Boar Street 12
boars 9–12, 32, 42, 45
Boar's Head Ceremony 10–11
Bobart, Jacob, the Elder 13–14
Bodleian Library 2, 23, 32, 41, 48, 49
Bodley, Thomas 32
Botanic Garden 9, 10, 13, 15, 45, 50
Brasenose College 5–6, 7
Buckland, Frank 44, 45
Buckland, William **43**, 43–4, 50
Buckley, John 27
buffalo 42, 48, **49**, 53
bulls 21, 22, 36, 45, 47
bush-babies 32

camels 40, **42**, 47
Carfax 1, 13
Carroll, Lewis (Charles Dodgson) 32, 33, 53
cats 2, 7, 33, 44, 45, 47, 53
Catte Street 6–7, 48
cattle 1, 3, 34, 35; *see also* bulls, cows, oxen
Chequers, The (pub) 40
choughs 17–18, **18**
Christ Church 12–13, 25, 33, 38, 40, 43, 44, 45
Christ Church Meadow 1, 3, 5, 18
cobras 32
cocks 21, 22, 36, **36**, 37
Copcot, John 10
Cornmarket 30
Corpus Christi College 7, 8, 15–16, 19, 24–7, 43
    sundial **15**, 15–16, **24**, **26**
    tortoises 25
Covered Market 29
cows 2, 13
crocodiles 2, 42
crows 2, 17, 36, **36**, 37

Danby Arch 13, 15
Darwin, Charles 44, 49, 50, 51
Daubeny, Charles 15, **43**, 44, 49–50
deer 4–5, 12, 35, 45, 48
d'Eglesfield, Robert 19–20
Deydras, John 7
Dodgson, Charles (Lewis Carroll) 32, 33, 53
dodos 1, 32, 33, 51, 53, **54**, 55
dogs 8–10, 38, 42, 43, 44, 45
    frieze **38**, 39

59

gargoyle 8–9, **9**
painting 46, **46**
dormice 32
doves 36, 55
dragons 2, 4, 30, 31, 32, 34, 40
Dragon School 30
ducks 35, 37; *see also* mallards

Eagle and Child, The (pub) 20
eagles 19, 20, 22, 30, 31, 35–6, 39, 42, 45
elephants 2, 4, 29, 35, 40, 43
  bench end **41**, 42
  frieze 48, **49**
emus 24, 32, 42
Examination Schools 38
Exeter College 19, 34

Fitzjames Arch 39, **39**
Fletcher, William 23
Folly Bridge 6, 23–4
Fox, Richard 8, 25, 26
foxes 7–8, **8**, 44
frogs 44, 45, 50, 52

Ganymede 20
gargoyles 1, 8–9, **9**, 32
geese 22, 34, 35, 36, **36**, 37
giraffes 40, 43
goats 10, 13–14, 45
Great Debate Plinth 51, **51**
griffins (gryphons) 21, 22, 23, 30–2, **31**, 35, 40
grotesques 32

Haida totem pole 52, **52**
hawks 40, 44
Headington Shark **27**, 27–8
Heine, Bill 27, 28
heraldry 1, 4, 8, 17, 22, 29, 30–1
hippos 40, 42
Hoare, Joseph 7
Holywell Street 32, 48

Hope, Frederick 51
horses 8, 12, 13, 15, 30, 34, 35, 42, 47, 53
Hugh of Fouilloy 2
Huxley, Thomas Henry 49, 50

Iffley Parish Church 35–6, **36**
Indian Institute 48–9, **49**
Inklings, The 20
Isidore of Seville 2, 29, 31

jackdaws 18, 44
Jesus College 7, 17, 19
John the Baptist, St 35–6, **38**, 38–9

Keble College 8
Kellogg College **37**, 37–8
Kettell Hall 6, **6**
Kybald Twychen 18–19, **19**

Lack, Andrew 52
Lady Margaret Hall 8
Lamb & Flag, The (pub) **14**, 14–15, 20
Lamb of God 14, **38**, 39
lambs 14, 42
  frieze **38**, 39
  pub sign **14**
  stained-glass window 36, **36**, 37
Leonardo da Vinci 15
leopards 6
Lewis, C. S. 20, 32, 34
Liddell, Alice, and sisters 33, 53
Lincoln College 27
Linge, Abraham van 27
lions 4, 6, 19, 22, 30–2, 34–40, 42, 45–7
  door knocker 6, **6**
  frieze 48, **49**
  golden half-lion 6, **6**
  heraldic crest 5, **5**
  royal coat of arms 4, 7, **29**
Lucretius 9, 48

Macdonald, Sir David 7–8

Magdalen Bridge 1, 13
Magdalen College 4–5, 12, 19, 23, 24, 25
Magpie Lane 18–19
magpies 18, 44
Mallard, William 23
mallards 20–3, 47
Mallard Song 20–3
marmots 45
martlets 17
mermaids and mermen 28–9, 32, 35
Merton College 14, 15, 19, 38, 39
    frieze **38**, 38–9
    roof boss 39, **39**
mice 2, 32, 33, 45, 50
Midgley, Graham 8–9, **9**
Molossian hounds 9
mongooses 32
monkeys 15, 45, 47, **50**
monsters 35, 36, 37, 40
Morrell's Brewery lion 6, **6**
Museum of the History of Science 53;
    see also Old Ashmolean Museum

New College 13, 32, 40
Noah's Ark 55
Northgate House 30

octopus jar 47, **47**
Old Ashmolean Museum (Museum of
    the History of Science) **43**, 43–4, 53
Old Black Horse Inn 13
Oriel College 18, 19
ostriches 24
otters 32
owls 24, 40, 41, 44, 53
    stained-glass window 36, **36**, 37
    sundial base **24**, 26
oxen **3**, 3–4, 36
Oxford Boys' School 3
Oxford City: coat of arms 3, 4, 35
Oxford Playhouse 40–1
Oxford Town Hall 4

Oxford University Museum of Natural
    History 1, 38, 43, 49–52
    dodo 1, 53, **54**
    plinth 51, **51**

peacocks 23, 28, 40, 53
Peel, Charles 40
pelicans 15–16, 24, 39, 42
    frieze **38**, 39
    sundial **15**, 15–16, **26**
Perch Inn 28
Piero di Cosimo 47, 48
Piper, John 36
Pitt Rivers Museum 32, **52**, 52–3
Pliny the Elder 2, 52
Pope, Sir Thomas 31
Port Meadow 1, 34–5
Pullman, Philip 34

Queen's College 10–12, 19–20, 32

rabbits **38**, 39, 44
Radcliffe Infirmary 28
ravens 2, **52**
Red Barn, The 40
'Red Lady' skeleton 50–1
Richmond Road: synagogue 55
Ruskin, John 38

Said Business School: bronze ox **3**, 3–4
St Edmund Hall 8, 17, 37
    gargoyle 8–9, **9**
    sundial 17–18, **18**
St Hilda's College 24–5, 29
St Hugh's College 16
St John's College 14, 20
St Mary's Church, Iffley 35–6, **36**
St Peter-in-the-East Church (St Edmund
    Hall Library) 8–9, **9**, 37
Scorpio (zodiac sign): roof boss 39, **39**
sharks **27**, 27–8, 40
sheep 40, 45, 47; *see also* lambs

Sheldonian Theatre 7, **29**, 32, 48
snakes 15, 24–5, 32, 42, 44, 45, 50
sphinxes 10, 35
Spotted Cow, The (Turf Tavern) 13
stags 4–5, 7, 48
swans 16, 22, 23–4, 40, 42, 45
swifts 17, 52

Talbot, Edward Stuart 8
Tenniel, John 33
Tiepolo, Giovanni Battista 47
tigers 42, 48
Tiglath Pileser (bear) 45
Tolkien, J. R. R. 1, 20, 32, 34
Tom Quad 33, 44
tortoises 25, 38, 42, 44, 45, 51
Tradescant, John, the Younger 53
Tree of Life **36**, 36–7
Trinity College 6, 31–2
   bookstand **31**
   tortoises 25
Triton (merman) 28
Trout Inn 28

Turf Tavern 13
Turnbull sundial **15**, 15–16, **24**, **26**
turtles 33, 44

Uccello, Paolo 47
unicorns 2, 29–30, 42
   frieze 38, **38**
   royal coat of arms 4, 7, **29**
University College 17, 20, 25

Wadham College 9, 19, 26
whales 27, 36, 42
Whitby 24–5
White Horse, The (pub) 13
Wilberforce, Samuel 49, 50
Wilkins, John 9, 26
Wolvercote, *see* Trout Inn
Wolvercote Common 34–5
Wood, Anthony à 23, 39
Worcester College:
   chapel **41**, 41–2, **42**
   coat of arms 17
   tortoise 25